Teardrops
to
Diamonds

HOW GOD'S LOVE TURNS
SORROW INTO JOY

Teardrops
to
Diamonds

CARL W. BERNER

AUGSBURG Publishing House • Minneapolis

TEARDROPS TO DIAMONDS

Library of Congress Catalog Card No. 83-70505
International Standard Book No. 0-8066-2011-0

Scripture quotations unless otherwise noted are from the Revised Standard Version of the Bible, copyright 1946, 1952, and 1971 by the Division of Christian Education of the National Council of Churches.

Additional scripture quotations are from the following translations:

KJ King James Version

LB The Living Bible, copyright 1971 by Tyndale House Publishers

NAS New American Standard Bible © The Lockman Foundation 1960, 1962, 1963, 1968, 1971, 1972, 1973

NEB The New English Bible. Copyright The Delegates of the Oxford University Press and The Syndics of the Cambridge University Press, 1961, 1970. Reprinted by permission.

TEV The Good News Bible, Today's English Version, copyright 1966, 1971, 1976 by American Bible Society. Used by Permission.

PHILLIPS The New Testament in Modern English, copyright 1958 by J. B. Phillips.

Photos: Philip Gendreau, 14, 35; Wallowitch, 19, 30; H. Armstrong Roberts, 24; Religious News Service, 42; Daniel D. Miller, 48; Strix Pix, 56; Elizabeth Wood, 61; William Bash, 66; Richard T. Lee, 71; Bob Taylor, 77; Camerique, 82; Eva Louma Photos, 87.

Manufactured in the United States of America

To my wife, whose loving care
has proved true Goethe's exquisite comment:
"Woman is God's compensation
for the loss of paradise."

Contents

Tribulation— for Better or for Worse?

God says to burden bearers: "When all kinds of trials and temptations crowd into your lives, don't resent them as intruders, but *welcome them as friends!*" (James 1:2 PHILLIPS).

Jesus said, "Blessed are you when people revile you and persecute you" (Matt. 5:11). Why does he say that? His answer: "Your reward is great in heaven."

Regardless of the reward, isn't that asking too much? To extend a glad hand of welcome to trials and tribulations? To rejoice under revilings and persecutions?

Ordinarily people do the opposite. They resent adversities. They grumble about getting what they call a "raw deal."

Some try to cover their pain with bravado. They put on a grin-and-bear-it stance. They dismiss every adversity as "just one of those things."

We're perhaps safe in saying that most people do not respond to trials and tribulations as God directs. They show no interest or intent to derive benefits from painful experiences.

For that they are much poorer. Their sorrows are wasted. God's intent is unrealized. Potentials of rich blessings are forfeited. Jesus' promise of a great "reward in heaven" is voided.

Believers have a different attitude toward cross-bearing. They know that "[God] may bring us sorrow, but his love for us is sure and strong. He takes no pleasure in causing us grief or pain" (Lam. 3:32-33 TEV).

What God allows in the lives of his children— bitter tears and heartbreak experiences—isn't easy to understand. But what God *does* with what he allows always makes good sense. He turns it all for good.

St. Paul attached great meaning and dignity to present trials, knowing what they would bring. "Whatever we may have to go through now is less than nothing compared with the magnificent future God has planned for us" (Rom. 8:18 PHILLIPS).

Tears are bearable when we know that God transforms them into diamonds. This he promised: "God will wipe away tears from all faces" (Isa. 25:8). "They that sow in tears shall reap in joy" (Ps. 126:5 KJ). Tears are liquid anguish. They speak a language God understands: "The

Lord has heard the sound of my weeping" (Ps. 6:8). God will remember them, "Put thou my tears in thy bottle! Are they not in thy book?" (Ps. 56:8)

Believers consider not only what they're going *through* but where they're going *to*. Jesus said, "You will be sorrowful, but your sorrow will turn into joy" (John 16:20). Like a clock that keeps on ticking in the thunderstorm, faith remains constant. We know what the outcome is—eternal joy in heaven.

GOD KNEW THE BEST

Sometime, when all life's lessons have been
    learned,
  When sun and stars forevermore have set,
The things which our weak judgment here have
    spurned,
  The things o'er which we grieved with lashes
    wet,
Will flash before us out of life's dark night,
  As stars shine most in deeper tints of blue;
And we shall see how all God's plans are right
  And how what seemed reproof was love most
    true.
But not today. Then be content, poor heart;
  God's plans like lilies pure and white unfold.
We must not tear the close-shut leaves apart.
  Time will reveal the calyxes of gold.

And, if through patient faith, we reach the land
Where tired feet, with sandals loosed, may rest;
Then we shall clearly see and understand,
I know that we shall say, *"God knew the best."*

Acknowledgments

My sincere thanks to the following people
for their invaluable suggestions:

Dr. Erwin W. Kurth

Dr. Lillie Andrews,
Christ College Irvine faculty

The Honorable William Dannemeyer,
member of Congress, Washington, D.C.

CHAPTER ONE

The Cross: World's Problem Solver

God forbid that I should glory,
save in the cross of our
Lord Jesus Christ.
Gal. 6:14 KJ

Anne Wendt, energetic and capable director of the Spastic Children's Foundation, revealed her success secret: "When I have a problem I go to the foot of the cross and stay there until I know God's plan for me."

The cross is the best known symbol in the world, and the simplest—two beams crossing each other. The vertical beam symbolizes an open path to the Father's heart. The horizontal beam, extending out over the world, is a symbol of God's grace for all.

Root Problems Crossed Out

Mankind's basic problems are resolved at the cross—the problem of sin and its curse, of death and its darkness, of hell and its terrors.

The victory was costly. Not gold or silver, but God himself. Dorothy Sayers put it crisply: "For whatever reasons, God chose to make man as he is —limited, suffering, subject to sorrows and death. But God had the honesty and courage to take his own medicine . . . he exacts nothing from man that he has not exacted from himself. He has himself gone through the whole human experience . . . including the worst horrors of pain and humiliation, defeat, despair, and death."

The cross is proof that God is for us. He is on our side. Under a picture of Christ on the cross a little girl wrote: "This is how much God loved me." Life's riddles, contradictions, pain, and anguish are rightly viewed against the backdrop of the cross.

Evil Turned into Good

In a way the cross was the greatest crime in history. It was maneuvered by Satan, who planted the idea of betrayal in Judas' heart. Satan moved the howling crowd to demand Jesus' death by crucifixion.

When Jesus died, Satan and his crew of terrorists held jubilee. The underworld went wild. But

God trumped the devil's ace. On the third day the grave was empty. The gravest crime was turned into the greatest blessing.

For God this is normal—turning evil into good. He's been doing that through the years.

Joseph was sold into slavery by his envious brothers. God turned that into good. Joseph became God's agent to liberate his people.

Paul bore in his body "the brand-marks of the Lord Jesus Christ." His bruises are now diadems.

Death, man's arch foe, has become a friendly porter at the gate of life.

To this day God is turning the bitter tears of his beloved children into glistening diadems, their sorrows into songs, their pain into gain, their agony into ecstacy.

Know What You Are

When your turn comes to face life's adversities, it is important that you know who you are and to whom you belong. By virtue of your faith union with the cross you can say:

I am a redeemed, baptized, forgiven, honored, loved child of God. I belong to the heavenly Father who has made me his child, to the divine Savior who gave his life for my salvation, to the Holy Spirit whose temple I am.

When life's path becomes shadowed and the valley grows dark, the heavenly Father whispers:

17

"My dear child, trust me. What I allow, however painful and hard to bear, will turn out for your good. I promise you that I am making you fit for the marriage banquet of the Lamb. I ask you to regard the hard knocks of life as a prelude to the high joys of heaven."

Life's Goal

To the question "Lord, what do you want for me?" God answers, "I want you to be with me forever in heaven." Jesus prayed: "Father, I want those whom you have given me to be with me" (John 17:24 PHILLIPS).

It was for "the joy that was set before him," the joy of having us forever at his side, that Jesus "endured the cross, despising the shame" (Heb. 12:2).

All God's actions concentrate on the goal of bringing us to eternal life. What he does in us, with us, to us, for us, is determined by his purpose to have us forever in his family.

Heaven is a holy place. Without holiness "no one will see the Lord" (Heb. 12:14). Our world is full of unholiness. "The whole world is in the power of the evil one" (1 John 5:19).

It follows that the children of God live in a state of tension. We are in combat against Satan, the evil world, our sinful flesh.

There is an impression abroad that faith in

Christ opens a charmed, trouble-free existence. Life with God is depicted as an easygoing, non-strenuous floating downstream. No one should get sick, at least no one should stay sick. Think positively, and you will live in constant sunshine.

A popular television preacher defines faith as "overcoming negative thoughts, building self-confidence, tapping the limitless possibilities within self." Not a word about sin, about the cross and forgiveness. Paul, Augustine, Luther, Wesley, and Walter A. Maier would have winced painfully to hear Christian faith explained like that.

Paul took his position under the cross. "God forbid that I should glory, save in the cross of my Lord Jesus Christ" (Gal. 6:14 KJ). No self-glorification, no self-righteousness, only the cross on which the Prince of glory died.

The supreme counterfeit in religion is a way to God other than God's way. God's way stands in sharp contrast to the boot-strap technique centering in the adulation of the perpendicular pronoun. Someone has defined Christianity as the 'I' crossed out. "Not I, but Christ," was Paul's slogan.

Jesus said, "If any man would come after me, let him deny himself, and take up his cross and follow me" (Matt. 16:24). Self must get out of the way if Christ is to have his way.

From the moment of his conversion, St. Paul considered himself a slave of Christ, under new

20

management. Christ, not he, was the center of his life. "The life I now live in the flesh I live by faith in the Son of God, who loved me and gave himself for me" (Gal. 2:20).

Faith Will See Us Through

God is not an impersonal, aloof force up in the sky. He is our heavenly Father. He loved us with an everlasting love. He is like a father with a mother's heart. "As one whom his mother comforts, so I will comfort you" (Isa. 66:13). No matter what his love and wisdom may have chosen for us, it was carefully planned for our good.

We strike from our dictionary such words as *fate, luck,* and *accident.* Christians do not believe that fate can plunge them into disaster, or that a black cat crossing in front of them is an ill omen, or that the stars or signs of the zodiac affect their lives for good or ill. Faith and fatalism cannot live in the same heart.

Every Christian can confidently and victoriously live with this assurance: I know that I am not exempt from life's adversities, but I also know and believe that nothing can strike me apart from the good and gracious will of my heavenly Father. Nothing can reach me before it passes him. His love is true and his knowledge of the future is perfect. When his plan for my life brings me to the shadowed path or the dark

21

valley, I know that even there I shall find some lovely flowers that grow only in the shade.

Trouble Is a Common Denominator

God won't let us get by without trouble. If he did, we would quit striving, questing, and struggling. Even a good Christian like St. Paul said, "We are troubled on every side" (2 Cor. 4:8 KJ).

One would expect troubles to be cut in half for Christians. They may, in fact, be doubled. Before our conversion we had only one person to take care of— our old self. Now there are two of us— the old self and the new self. Our "old man," as Paul calls him, is always stirring up trouble. The "new man" is contending to keep the upper hand.

"The Lord disciplines those whom he loves" (Heb. 12:6 NEB). Sometimes, when the hurt is deep and lasts a long time, we may wish that he didn't love us so much. But we really can't mean that. He cannot leave us as we are; he loves us too much for that.

The love that allows us to get down with crippling arthritis, disabling muscular dystrophy, painful angina, and heartbreak in the family, seems a dubious kind of love. It doesn't seem right that godly people are wracked with pain, while some who don't care about God go scot free.

The psalm writer, Asaph, nearly lost his faith over this riddle. God was piling it on him. Others were sailing merrily on with nary a struggle. At last he came to victory. He realized that God does not close his books at the end of every day, but will close them eventually. He knew that his troubles were for triumph. He snuggled into the arms of God. He exulted in the knowledge that God was dealing with him as a son: "Whom have I in heaven but Thee? And besides Thee, I desire nothing on earth. My flesh and heart may fail; But God is the strength of my heart and my portion forever" (Ps. 73:25-26 NAS). A person having God is rich, no matter what his or her troubles are. A person not having God is poor, no matter how many troubles he or she escapes.

When life tumbles in, we can express an action of faith or of doubt. In one case we win; in the other we lose. God is always nudging us toward faith. "Do not fear, for I have redeemed you; I have called you by name; you are mine . . . and I love you . . . Do not fear, for I am with you" (Isa. 43:1-5 NAS).

Have you ever heard anything more gracious and fatherly than that? Your response: "I am his. I belong to him. He will take care of me." That's true reality. And that kind of reality is more important than the doctor telling you that you have a dreadful malady. Such reality gives you the confidence of the Lord's saving power in your life. Fear vanishes in the face of it. Faith's light dispels the shadows.

Chastening Makes Us Chaste

Pain, suffering, adversity, and affliction exercise a ministry of cleansing and renewal. It is when they are crushed that flowers release their richest fragrance. Gold is flung into the furnace to reach its full purity and value.

God allows fiery trials so that impurities such as obstinacy, impatience, and self-centeredness might be burned out. Trials sweep away the debris that has cluttered life with things that hide God. The shore is swept clean by the storm, and we get a new experience of the ocean of God's grace.

Our eyes are drawn from the glamor of sin to the beauty of godliness. Our ears become less attentive to earth's music, and more attuned to the "Hallelujah Chorus." Our goals shift from earthly tinsel to heavenly treasure. Our feet incline less to the byways of the world and more to the road that leads home.

Trials for Triumph

It is true, and God admits it, that "for the moment all discipline seems painful rather than pleasant" (Heb. 12:11). There's no fun in facing "the slings and arrows of outrageous fortune." But the gain God has in mind far outweighs the pain. It takes a lot of faith to join Paul in saying,

25

"We glory in tribulation." Once we reach that level we'll join him in the resolve, "In everything give thanks." We learn to thank God for thorns and roses, for gloomy days and bright days, and for dark valleys and sunny mountain peaks.

Paul tells us how to look beyond the trials to the triumphs. "Though our outward humanity is in decay, yet day by day we are inwardly renewed. Our troubles are slight and short-lived, and their outcome an eternal glory which outweighs them far" (2 Cor. 4:16 NEB).

Out of Agony Comes Ecstacy

There is an old story about a violin maker who searched all his life for a certain kind of wood from which he could make violins of unusual beauty and tone. At last he found what he searched for—wood taken from the timberline, the last stand of trees in the mountains, 12,000 feet above sea level. Here winds blow so hard that the bark on the wind side has hardly any chance to grow. All the trees are bowed down to the ground, brought to their knees, as it were, in order to live. There the world's best wood for violins is found. From the agonized trees are made violins of velvety tone and clear resonance.

So it is with affliction-tested believers. Their refined and tempered spirit produces tranquil

26

melodies of inner peace. Tribulation produces the grace notes of life.

From her sick bed following radical surgery Ruth Anderson, member of St. Mark's Church, Anaheim, California, sounded lovely grace notes: "God is closer to me than ever before. Though he now has taken away my physical health, he has given me an experience of spiritual healing and victory. Before God dealt with me in this way I took almost everything for granted—the church, the Bible, my health, even my husband and family. Through this illness God brought about a change in my life. He is nearer and dearer to me than ever before." Ruth now lives with her Lord in glory.

Sometimes church members grow cold and careless. There is no fervor and fire in them. They can't get excited over anything God says or does. Then God sends winds of adversity to shake them up. They discover the enduring values that cannot be shaken. And for that discovery they will be eternally thankful.

On a television program, children who experienced catastrophic illness told their story. One boy said, "Before this happened to me I had a mean spirit and was hard to live with. I fought with my brother and gave my parents a hard time. Because of my sickness the whole family is different. Now we cooperate with each other and work together." A sixteen-year-old girl said, "This is the best thing that ever happened to me. I am no longer the selfish person I was. I am interested in others, and I try to love everyone." Another girl said, "I used to have a rebellious spirit and was very selfish. My sickness changed all that. My parents and friends have noticed the change that has come over me. I have faith in God and love for people. Too bad God had to be so rough on me to bring this about, but I'm glad he did."

CHAPTER TWO

Cross Bearers, Crown Wearers

*He will receive the crown of
life which God has promised to
those who love him.*

James 1:12

David, the "man after the heart of God," was
an inveterate cross bearer. He was persecuted by
Saul, cursed by Doeg, betrayed by Sheba, maligned
by Nadab, derided by Shimei, and mocked by his
son Absalom. His strong faith in God carried him
through trials and turmoils. "I have heard the
slander of many . . . they devised to take away
my life. But I trusted in thee, O, Lord. I said,
Thou art my God. My times are in thy hand"
(Ps. 31:13-14 KJ).

"My times are in thy hand." What rich consolation is wrapped up in these words! When storm

clouds threaten, when sickness strikes, when "doubts assail and fears annoy," when death draws near, we are in the hands of God. That's the safest and best place in all the world to be.

In a famous speech Edward VIII, king of England, had these memorable words: "I said to the man who stood at the gate of the year, 'Give me a light for the unknown path ahead.' But he said to me, 'Take hold of my hand, that is better than a light or a known way.' " David knew this: "Thy true love stands high above me" (Ps. 86:13 NEB). In all that happened he saw some movement of the Father's love.

Rise above Troubles

One of our common mistakes is that we live with our troubles. We live with them instead of above them. We allow them to get inside us, control us, toss us around, and churn up our emotions. In short our troubles overtake us. This is ruinous.

When things go wrong, we ought not go wrong with them. That's the time to go right. David knew what to do. "My fears looked unto the Lord and were lightened" (Ps. 34:5). His fears were there, but so was his faith.

To retain composure and control we each need to say to ourselves: "Things around me have

31

changed, but I have not changed. Nothing in me has changed. I am still the person I was before. I will not let adversity tear me apart and turn me into a different person. Things may be shaking all around me, but I know the promise God made to his trusting child, 'Nothing shall shake him . . . Bad news shall have no terrors for him, because his heart is steadfast, trusting in the Lord.' (Ps. 112:6-7 NEB)."

Troubles can bless or burn. They bring a blessing when they inspire the spirit's flight upward. They burn and blister when they are pent up within. Here's a good resolve: I will not let troubles diminish my faith, shatter my peace, and destroy my composure. I will put the full weight of trust on God's trustworthy promise, "Thou wilt keep him in perfect peace, whose mind is stayed on thee" (Isa. 26:3 KJ).

In God's Arms

A weathered Christian told of a dream in which he saw himself walking with the Lord on the seashore. In his dream long-forgotten scenes of his life were recalled. In each scene he saw two sets of footprints, his own and the Lord's. Then something strange happened: there was a scene showing only one set of footprints. And that particular scene covered some heartbreaking experiences during a trying and tearful time of his life. He said to the Lord, "When we started together, you promised to stay with me all the way. Why did you forsake me when I needed you most?"

The Lord replied, "My dear child, I did not forsake you. There was only one set of footprints in the days of your dire need because then I carried you."

Crosses Are Tailor-Made

An ancient legend tells of a sign over the door of the carpenter shop in Nazareth where Jesus worked with his father: OUR YOKES FIT. To prevent chafing and injury, every yoke had to be fitted to the neck of the oxen.

When God selects a cross for us, it is tailored to our individuality, "Let everyone take up his cross," Jesus said. The cross God has chosen for you is neither too light nor too heavy. It is exactly right.

In an old legend a woman complained that her cross was too heavy for her. The Lord took her cross from her, then led her to a field of many crosses, and said, "Go and select a cross that you feel is right for you." The woman made her choice. Fully satisfied with her selection she said, "I have found a cross I can bear, one just right for me." When she picked it up, she saw that it was her very own cross, the one she had rejected.

A Cross Now, a Crown Then

There is no Christian life without a cross. Neither is there a cross apart from God's power to turn it into a crown. Whenever Jesus spoke of his death, he spoke also of his victory over it. In this we should follow his example. The contemplation of our cross or death ought always to include the prospect of the promised crown in glory everlasting.

A cross rejected is Satan's instrument of torture. God's yoke never fits a stiff neck. A cross thoughtfully and thankfully accepted becomes Christ's gentle yoke of training for glory. After the tears of Gethsemane came the triumph of the resurrection. After the cross came the crown. "Weeping may tarry for the night, but joy comes with the morning" (Ps. 30:5).

Now shadows, then sunshine. Now tears, then diamonds. "Many are the afflictions of the righteous, but the Lord delivers him out of them all" (Ps. 34:19).

The early Christians marched to their death with courage and dignity. They were confident that their gain would far outweigh their pain. Looking back now, comparing their former agony with their present ecstacy they are saying, "We would do it all over again. So great is our present glory that the foregoing suffering isn't worthy to be compared with it."

No matter what life threw at him, David knew that one door was always open. "I call upon God; and the Lord will save me" (Ps. 55:16).

In the suffering of his Son, God drew closest to us, and we draw closest to him. One saint asserted: "We are never so close to God as we are when his hand is heavy upon us." Then it is close enough to grasp. "Friend, hold on," God is saying, "Hang on, and don't let go. Together we'll make it."

Get the Vision!

Every year more than 30 million Americans get sick and enter hospitals. On the debit side this spells pain, anguish, disruption of family life, financial loss. What about the credit side? What are the gains? Do the gains match the losses?

Whatever the cost, illness isn't always a liability. It is definitely an asset when it brings blessings which otherwise would not be achieved.

To turn loss into capital we need these good-sense, God-pleasing attitudes and resolves:

We can't do much about the cost, however excessive, but we are determined to achieve the highest profit.

We know that the price will be right if the gain is right.

We will not ask, "Lord, what are you trying to do *to* us?" but will ask "Lord, what are you trying to do *for* us?"

We will keep in mind this important truth: whatever draws us closer to God, however painful or costly, is a blessing for which we will be eternally thankful. What we are going *through* is softened and sanctified by what we are going *to*.

Your Thorn in the Flesh

Paul had what he called "a thorn in the flesh." It was a physical affliction of some kind. Scholars have variously held that it was malaria, epilepsy, migraine headaches, chronic eye infection. Paul regarded this "thorn" as "a messenger of Satan, to harass me" (2 Cor. 12:7). God allowed it, he felt, "to keep me from being too elated." Three times Paul asked the Lord to rid him of this affliction. But the Lord answered every time, "My grace is all you need; power comes to its full strength in weakness" (2 Cor. 12:9 NEB). Paul received strength to be content with God's answer: "I have cheerfully made up my mind to be proud of my weaknesses, because they mean a deeper experience of the power of Christ" (2 Cor. 12:10 PHILLIPS).

The thorn came from Satan. All physical maladies do. Having wrought sin, Satan is responsible for every flaw and imperfection—physical, moral, spiritual. Man was sin's victim, not its designer.

God turned the thorn of pain into an occasion for gain. Paul saw how it worked out: "God's strength is made perfect in weakness." Paul became strong when, in his weakness, he turned to the Lord for strength. "I can do all things in him who strengthens me" (Phil. 4:13).

Every child of God has some kind of "thorn in the flesh"—eye trouble, ear trouble, lung trouble, heart troubles, arthritis, neuritis, rheumatic fever, migrain headaches—any one or more of 1600 known physical ills.

With valiant Paul we resolve: "I will not let any 'thorn' diminish my faith or shatter the peace of God. When Satan attacks I will say what Jesus said: 'The Prince of this world approaches. He has no rights over me' (John 14:30 NEB)."

Satan is mighty, but God is almighty.

CHAPTER THREE

Four Pillars
to Cling to

When the earth rocks . . .
I make its pillars firm.
Ps. 75:3 NEB

In his Word God provided four strong and firm pillars of truth to cling to against the fierce winds of adversity. On these unshakable pillars life is built strong and true.

Pillar One:
I Am Here by God's Appointment

Paul saw God's love and authority in every step of his life. So should we, knowing that "every affliction comes with a message from the heart of God."

When Paul came to the water's edge at Troas, he didn't know which way to turn. God answered his call for direction. In a night vision he saw a man in Macedonian attire beckoning, "Come over here and help us!" Obedient to the heavenly vision, Paul, with Silas, Timothy, and Luke, crossed the sea and headed toward Philippi. Here, as usual, his preaching stirred up violent opposition. He and Silas were beaten, then imprisoned, with hands and feet in stocks. Instead of giving way to dejection and self-pity, they lifted up their voices in praise to God. They knew they were there by God's appointment. They looked beyond their troubles to God, who, they were sure, would do something. He did! There was a violent quake, the earth rocked, Paul and Silas stood firm on the truth of God's promise. The jailer and his family were converted. The church in Philippi was founded. That's why they had come in the first place. Their trust in God was vindicated.

Paul's method was to look beyond the circumstances to his sovereign God who is above circumstance. From his prison in Rome he wrote to the Ephesians, "I am a prisoner of Jesus Christ." Not, "I am a prisoner of Rome . . . or of Nero," but "of Jesus Christ."

A point of view can make a big difference. One person views imprisonment as pain and bad luck; another views it as privilege and opportunity.

His experiences taught Paul an important lesson: "I have learned, in whatever state I am, to be content" (Phil. 4:11). Whatever life threw at him—it didn't make much difference what it was —God would make it all work out for good.

To the Philippians he wrote from prison: "What has happened to me has really served to advance the gospel" (Phil. 1:12). For Paul every dark cloud had a silver lining. His extremity was God's opportunity. He was chained to a soldier: that was the extremity. The soldier was a person for whom Christ died: that was the opportunity. Members of "Caesar's household" were converted through Paul's prison preaching.

In every life situation our extremity, too, is God's opportunity.

> I begged him to let this cup pass from me,
> But he did not, so I tilted it to see,
> If there were within a grace,
> To heal my pride and ease the pain,
> A gift from God, to make me whole again!
> And love flamed out, as endless as the sky.
> My cross became a banner, flying high.

Every dark experience yields a bit of God's light.

Pillar Two: I Am in God's Keeping

Peter describes believers as those "who by God's power are guarded through faith for a salvation

ready to be revealed in the last time. In this you rejoice, though now for a little while you may have to suffer various trials, so that the genuineness of your faith, more precious than gold which though perishable is tested by fire, my redound to praise and glory and honor at the revelation of Jesus Christ" (1 Peter 1:5-7).

There is a divine "if need be" behind God's dealing with us. Only when we need it does the heavenly Physician use his scalpel. He may hurt us, but he will not injure us. For God's children there are no needless tears.

Lord,
help me not to dread
what might happen,
not to worry about
what could happen,
but to accept what does happen,
because you care for me.
    DOROTHY MOFFITT

"God is faithful, and he will not let you be tempted beyond your strength, but with the temp tation will also provide the way of escape, that you may be able to endure it" (1 Cor. 10:13).

Robert Louis Stevenson said: "For me Christianity is summarized in five words; we have a caring God."

Simon Peter exhorts, "Cast all your anxieties on him, for he cares about you" (1 Peter 5:7).

We have a caring God. He proved this by sending his Son into the world to bail us out of our predicament and to bring us the joy of forgiveness and the hope of everlasting life. Having given us the major gift, he won't hesitate to give us minor gifts. "He who did not spare his own Son, but gave him up for us all, will he not also give us all things with him?" (Rom. 8:32).

The Living Bible has this paraphrase: "Even when walking through the dark valley of death I will not be afraid, for you are close beside me, guarding, guiding me all the way" (Ps. 23:4). What iron enters the blood when we know that Jesus is with us all the way! He promised: "I will never leave thee nor forsake thee" (Heb. 13:5 KJ). There are dangers and hazards all around. Cunning and designing enemies lurk in the shadows. We need fear none of them. With us is One who is stronger than Satan's entire corps of fiends. Enemies against us are strong; God is stronger.

"This I know, that God is for me," David sang (Ps. 56:9). This is one of the most delightful verses in the Bible. We ought to take it with us wherever we go. David did. The heading of Psalm 56 shows that David's conviction came to him in a day when things looked dark. Then light blazed into his soul: "God knows what I am going through. My tears are in his bottle. This I know, God is for me."

44

Pillar Three:
I Am Here under God's Training

No school in the world offers better training than God's school of adversity. In this school we learn by experience. Experience is often a stern—even cruel—method of teaching. It gives the examination first, then teaches the lesson. Undoubtedly it is the most effective of all methods of teaching and learning.

St. Paul valued his training in the school of experience: "We rejoice in our sufferings, knowing that suffering produces endurance, and endurance produces character, and character produces hope" (Rom. 5:3-4).

Sometimes God makes us helpless in order to help us. That's what he did for Marianne Lueth, now associated with Lutheran Bible Translators, who writes: "God knew what he had to do to get me to do what he wanted. I asked him to forgive me for my trifling and to take my life totally into his hands. This he has done. I regard it a privilege to be chosen as his child and heir. I am thankful that he loves me so much that he is refining me toward improvement."

God puts us into the fire "so that the genuineness of your faith, more precious than gold which though perishable is tested by fire, may redound to praise and glory and honor at the revelation of Jesus Christ" (1 Peter 1:7).

"What makes this set of china so much more expensive than the other?" asked a customer. "Because it has been put through the fire twice," the clerk answered. "You see, in this one the flowers are on a yellow bank; in that one, they are on white background. This one had to be put through the fire a second time for the richer design."

Some cross bearers are being doubly tried in the fire that they may receive a double blessing.

AFFLICTION'S BLESSING

Only melted gold is minted,
Clouded skies are rainbow-tinted,
Only wax that has been softened takes the die;
Plastic clay the potter useth
Tempered steel the town smith chooseth,
Clear the reason; none the need
to question why.
Untilled soil is never seeded,
Fallowed fields are never weeded,
Reaping never comes where seed has not
been sown.
Skill awaits the toiling fingers,
Comes where patient effort lingers;
To the humble, earnest seeker truth is known.
To the humble soul God calleth,
In the softened heart seed falleth,
Richest fruits of righteousness
the sowing grace.

Of the plastic will God maketh
Vessel that his image taketh
Tempered lives he chooseth for the
highest place.

H. V. ANDREWS

An uncut diamond is unattractive. No one
would think of wearing it. A diamond is brilliant
because so many facets are cut upon its surface,
and every facet reflects its own ray of light. It is
the cutting that beautifies the gem. After it is
cut, the diamond glows with every color of the
rainbow.

Often in sickness and trial one facet after another is cut and polished on the diamond of self,
making it luminous and radiant. We are like
rough diamonds that God takes into his workshop
for cutting and polishing, reflecting his glory.

"We . . . are being changed into his likeness from
one degree of glory to another" (2 Cor. 3:18).

When the heavenly Sculptor keeps on chipping
away at us, and it seems that we've had more
than our share of pain and anguish, we may feel
like saying: "Stop, Lord, I've had enough of this!"
But we really can't mean it, for that would be
asking him to cease loving us. If we truly believe
that "whom the Lord loveth he chasteneth" we
will not ask, when his chastenings fall, "Lord,
what are you doing *to* me?" but, "Lord, what are
you doing *for* me?"

47

A silversmith was gazing intently on the molten silver that he was stirring in a crucible.

"Why do you look so intently on the silver?" a friend asked.

The craftsman replied, "When I see my face reflected in it, then the silver is ready to receive the imprint of the coin."

The heavenly Silversmith will keep us in the fire until we reflect his image. The ultimate purpose of the salvation drama is to restore in us the beauty of the divine image. God has chosen us "to be conformed to the image of his Son" (Rom. 8:29).

Pillar Four: I Am Here for God's Time

Let not tomorrow's burdens rob us of today's strength. "Stay out of tomorrow!" Jesus said in effect. Take one day at a time. We're not strong enough to carry more than one day's burdens. Today is ours; tomorrow may never come. If it does come, God will still be alive.

Each day our faith can lean hard on this promise. Today is ours. Over yesterday God has spread the cloak of his forgiving mercy. Over tomorrow he has written words of hope and promise. Yesterday's mercy and tomorrow's promise inspire today's trust.

Each day we write the story of today. We dip our pen in the blue of God's love, and write in the

49

gold of his promises. This makes each day an adventure with him.

God taught Lydia Edson, a long-time personal friend, the secret of giving to each day a heart of faith and courage. She tells her story: "My daughter Katie now 50, has been ill with Friedrich's Disease since she was five. She has been bedridden the last 15 years. This demands a daily seven-hour ministry of special care. God is giving me strength to carry on. His sustaining grace is new every hour. I don't understand all that he allows, but I do understand his promise to make everything turn out right. He knows how to turn tears into triumph and sorrow into joy. I thank God that I am being drawn closer to him. Nothing is better than that."

One saint discovered nuggets of gold on the stormy path. He wrote:

> For every hill I've had to climb,
>> For every stone that bruised my feet,
> For all the blood and sweat and grime,
>> For blinding storms and burning heat,
> My heart sings but a grateful song—
>> These were the things that made me strong!

> For all the heartaches and the tears,
>> For all the anguish and the pain,
> For gloomy days and fruitless years,
>> And for the hopes that lived in vain,

I do give thanks, for now I know
   These were the things that helped me grow!

'Tis not the softer things of life
   Which stimulate man's will to strive;
But bleak adversity and strife
   Do most to keep men's will alive.
O'er rose-strewn paths the weaklings creep,
   But brave hearts dare to climb the steep.

Another courageous cross bearer testified: "When severe illness struck me down, I did what the Scriptures direct. I confessed my sin and prayed for healing (James 5:16) . When my prayer for physical healing was delayed, I accepted the truth that God doesn't always grant physical healing at once. But another truth shone like a light in my spirit. I realized that God had granted me a different kind of healing. He healed me spiritually and emotionally. The wonderful assurance of spiritual healing compensated me richly for the physical distress I was suffering. So, instead of losing my faith because God did not grant me physical healing, I now have a stronger faith than ever before. God answered my prayer by giving me something better than physical healing. He gave me a joyful, radiant faith in his love and wisdom, a gift that will endure forever. In a way he did answer my prayer for bodily healing. He said, 'Wait a while, I promise that I will renew your body to purest health in the coming new world.'

I praise and glorify God for what he has done for me. And I will do what he directs, 'Wait for the Lord; be strong and let your heart take courage' (Ps. 27:14)."

Here is a great word to share with your Christian friends who are ill: even if God doesn't heal you from your present sickness, he will use it to make you fit and ready for the eternal healing in his heavenly home.

The words of James are right on the beam: "When all kinds of trials and temptations crowd into your lives, my brothers, don't resent them as intruders, but welcome them as friends!" (James 1-2 PHILLIPS) .

CHAPTER FOUR

Seven Steps of Victory over Adversity

*By thy saving power, O God,
lift me high above my pain
and my distress.*
Ps. 69:29 NEB

Step One: Engage the Mind, Not the Emotions

God says, "Gird up your minds" (1 Peter 1:13). Set your mind on serious thinking. "For as he thinks within himself, so he is" (Prov. 23:7 NAS). Don't let your emotions take over.

Sound thinking directs us to regard the Holy Spirit as the best Counselor, the most successful of all Psychiatrists. This Author of truth and wisdom prescribes, "Don't let the world around you squeeze you into its mold, but let God remold your minds from within" (Rom. 12:2 PHILLIPS).

When it comes to right thinking, God's children have an advantage over others. Of us the Holy Spirit says, "You have the mind of Christ," which means that we adopt his attitude, follow his method, do his work, live in his will.

This is our endeavor. But we discover a gap between what we want and what we do. We can say, as did Paul: "I delight in the law of God . . . but I see in my members another law at war with the law of my mind" (Rom. 7:22-23).

This failure to match his attainments with his resolutions brought Paul to the edge of despair. "It is an agonizing situation, and who on earth can set me free from the clutches of my own sinful nature? I thank God there *is* a way out through Jesus Christ our Lord" (Rom. 7:24 PHILLIPS). The way out of every sin and failure is Christ's grace.

"God's divine power has given us everything we need to live a truly religious life" (2 Peter 1:3 TEV).

The alternatives are clear: "To set the mind on the flesh is death, but to set the mind on the Spirit is life and peace" (Rom. 8:6).

Secular counselors fall flat when they are not aware of the conflict between spirit and flesh. If they are wrong about our nature, it follows that they will be wrong about answers to our problems.

An adequate definition of what we truly are must take into account our inborn depravity. But if we knew only our depravity, we would run to the nearest hole and dive in.

We praise our beneficent God that we know not only our total loss in sin; we know also our complete redemption in Christ.

Instead of being totally discouraged by what the world has come to, we are encouraged by what has come into the world through our Lord Jesus Christ, the Great Liberator who gave his luminous promise, "If the Son makes you free, you will be free indeed" (John 8:36) .

It is a radical mistake to let emotions do our thinking for us. Emotions have no intelligence of their own. In themselves they cannot distinguish between right and wrong, fact and fancy.

Right thinking produces right emotions; wrong thinking produces wrong emotions.

Paul, an expert in Christian living, offers a list of do's and don'ts with their predictable results. Sow to the flesh by living in strife, envy, wrath, lust—and you'll reap a harvest of death. Sow to the Spirit by living in joy, peace, love, gentleness, goodness, kindness and you'll reap a harvest of life (Gal. 5:16-25) .

We were made for righteousness, not for sin. Righteousness always works out right; sin never does.

History and human experience prove that sin blights and burns. It begets mental, spiritual, physical, and social ills. Sin is the enemy of God and man. God declares it: "He who sins against me injures himself. All those who hate me love death" (Prov. 8:36 NAS).

If you were to ask your body to give you some honest answers, you may be in for a big surprise.

Perhaps your body would say, "The person I live with is giving me a rough time. He is always stirring up errant emotions, putting my nerves on edge, sending my glands on a rampage, filling me with dread, doubt, and worry. In short, he makes me sick."

You are to be congratulated if your body would say: "The person I live with brings me delight, joy, happiness. He always looks at the bright side of life, lives in the joy of faith, in the inspiration of love, in the courage of hope, and in the happiness of peace. Together we make a great team."

Doctors recognize the link between emotions and health. They know that one out of three hospital beds is occupied by psychiatric patients. They prescribe sedatives and tranquilizers, but that only slows down the thinking which controls emotions. When the drug wears off, the old disorders recur.

Victory over upsetting experiences requires thinking with "the mind of Christ," and keeping emotions in line with such thinking.

57

Step Two:
Anchor Yourself to God's Word

Feelings and emotions are like the ebb and flow of the sea. God's Word is our unshakeable anchor. Martin Luther said, "In time of trial we should rest not on our feelings, but on the Word of God."

The Word of God is the most reliable source of help in the world. It offers the best answers, gives the best advice, and provides a sure foundation. On this foundation we can place the full weight of trust without risk.

In turbulent times some turn for help to the zodiac, some to fortunetellers, some to cults. They never find the help they need.

One unique quality of the Word is that it offers at all times help for every need. The Word gives us help from trouble, but "vain is the help of man!" (Ps. 108:12).

Lloyd C. Douglas, a famous American author, enjoyed visiting an old violin teacher whose home-spun wisdom he found refreshing. One morning he walked into the old man's studio and asked, "What's the good word today?" Putting down his violin, the teacher stepped over to a tuning fork suspended from a cord. Upon striking it a sharp blow, he commented, "There's the good word for today. That, my friend, is the musical note A. It was A yesterday, it is A today, and it will be A next week and for a thousand years."

In the midst of change God has his fixed reference points. When all else crumbles, the Word stands fixed and firm.

David resolved: "The Lord is my portion; I promise to keep thy words" (Ps. 119:57). He who stands or falls by the Word will never fall.

Man's thoughts are like a vapor of smoke, but God's Word is a mountain of granite. It will stand longer than El Capitan in Yosemite Park. "Heaven and earth will pass away," Jesus said. "My words will never pass away" (Matt. 24:35 NEB).

God's Word does God's work. "I shall not return to Me empty, without accomplishing what I desire" (Isa. 55:11 NAS). Where the Word is, there God is. Where God is, there is help. Job observed, "By his light I walked through darkness" (Job 29:3).

David said that he would have fallen apart had not God's Word held him. "If thy law had not been my delight, I should have perished in my affliction" (Ps. 119:92).

When Nazi soldiers came to arrest Bishop Berggrav, a friend whispered in his ear, "Remember 1 Peter 3:14."

The bishop recounted: "I did not at all remember 1 Peter 3:14. I had no idea what it was about. While sitting in the car between two soldiers, I took out my pocket New Testament and found the verse. I think I never in my life experienced such a change of mind. I read the verse 'Be not afraid of their terror, neither be troubled, but sanctify the Lord God in your hearts.' I did indeed pray that Christ should be sanctified in my heart. When I was taken before the court I had a calm mind. Every trembling and every fear went away. I felt safe and secure." That was all he needed to face the ensuing trials victoriously.

The Word held Iranian hostage Kathryn Koob. She was the one who sang the Christmas hymn, "Away in a Manger," over world television. This is what she wrote: "Through those monotonous 444 days in prison these Bible verses from Psalm 118 were my anchor of hope: 'I shall not die, but live, and declare the works of the Lord. The Lord hath chastened me sore: but he hath not given me over unto death.' All through those trying days I thought of God as a pillar of support and strength."

The Word revived Tim Wampler. When this talented young man lay critically ill, the Word of God brought him back to his childhood faith. His mother, Molly, recalled how it happened: "One day Tim asked me to bring him his old Bible story book, which he had used in grade school. As he was unable to hold the book, I read to him. The Word did the work. It restored Tim's faith. He again claimed its precious promises. Through his fervent Christian witness his young Jewish roommate was led to salvation. As the end drew near,

God gave him a vision of the coming glory: 'Look mom,' he said, 'Look—it's too wonderful for words. I've never seen anything like it.' So Tim's soul winged its way home. He is forever safe with God."

The Word brought light into the dark night of a pastor friend in Texas. He tells his experience: "When the doctor gave his grim verdict of terminal cancer, my knees buckled and my spirit sank low. After a ministry of nearly 50 years, hope for a few years of health in retirement came to a sudden crash. There were days of agonizing emotional upheaval, tearful anxiety, bitter soul searching. Thereafter I experienced an almost sudden turnabout. An old country pastor came to my bedside, opened his Bible, and read these words of St. Paul from 2 Cor. 12:7-9 kj: 'There was given to me a thorn in the flesh, the messenger of Satan to buffet me, lest I should be exalted above measure. For this thing I besought the Lord thrice, that it might depart from me. And he said unto me, My grace is sufficient for thee; for my strength is made perfect in weakness. Most gladly therefore will I rather glory in my infirmities, that the power of Christ may rest upon me.' That did it. Those words brought light into my spirit. They continue to be my song in the night. I am holding them, and they are holding me."

The Word held George Steinbeck, former chaplain of Good Shepherd Home of the West. Following a violent car collision that resulted in multiple fractures and massive internal injuries, Pastor George experienced one crisis after another in his seven months of hospitalization. Again and again hope for his recovery was all but abandoned. He was ready to depart and be with Christ. But God heard the thousands of prayers on behalf of his faithful servant. Now, eight years later, George is up and around, enjoying years of well-deserved retirement with his wife, Hazel, in the lovely setting of their home in Paso Robles, California. What sustained this valiant soldier of the cross in those trying years? He explains: "I found comfort in the Scriptures that my faithful wife read to me constantly. One day a Christian nurse overheard me saying, 'God is our refuge and strength, a very present help in trouble.' 'Oh, that's beautiful,' she said, 'God gives strength day by day.' She hand-lettered those words on a card which remained posted over my bed. And those words remain engraved in my heart, and by his grace they will remain there until the road leads home."

When it comes to power, nothing can match God's Word and the Holy Spirit resident in it. Through his tears Jeremiah wrote: "Thy word is joy and happiness to me" (Jer. 15:16 NEB). When the world is bitter, the Word is sweet. The Word has power to get holy things started and to keep them going. The inner enrichment by the

Word has the same results as being filled with the Holy Spirit.

The Word gives us a new point of view. It replaces negative attitudes with the characteristics and attitudes of Christ. It changes both internal attitudes and external conduct. It gives attitudes that have altitude.

The two Emmaus disciples made a big mistake. Like many of us, they left home without taking with them God's credit card—the holy Word. For this failure they paid dearly. When rumors reached them about Christ's grave being empty, they sank into deep gloom. All hope fled. Jesus knew how upset they were; that signaled his mission of mercy. First Jesus led them to the Word. "O foolish men, and slow of heart to believe," he said. "Was it not necessary that the Christ should suffer these things and enter into his glory?" (Luke 24:25-26).

Jesus knew where they had failed. They were joyless because they were Wordless. Either they had forgotten or ignored what Jesus had said about his death and rising the third day. Had they remembered and believed this promise they would have exclaimed upon receiving word of the empty grave, "Praise God, it has happened! He said he would rise. Now he has risen! Glory, hallelujah!"

David carried with him memorized Word portions. For him the Word had ethically antiseptic value. "I have laid up thy Word in my heart, that I might not sin against thee" (Ps. 119:11).

God says, "Take with you words" (Hosea 14:2). Here are some words to take with you wherever you go. Hold them and they will hold you!

"The unfolding of thy words gives light" (Ps. 119:130).

"Thy word is a lamp to my feet and a light to my path" (Ps. 119:105).

"I revere thy commandments, which I love" (Ps. 119:48).

"This I know, that God is for me" (Ps. 56:9).

"If God is for us, who is against us?" (Rom. 8:31).

"Cast all your anxieties on him, for he cares about you" (1 Peter 5:7).

"I am with you always, to the close of the age" (Matt. 28:20).

"My grace is sufficient for you" (2 Cor. 12:9).

"For to me to live is Christ, and to die is gain" (Phil. 1:21).

"The Lord is my portion" (Ps. 119:57).

We can place the full weight of our trust on God's promise: "My Word . . . shall accomplish that which I purpose" (Isa. 55:11).

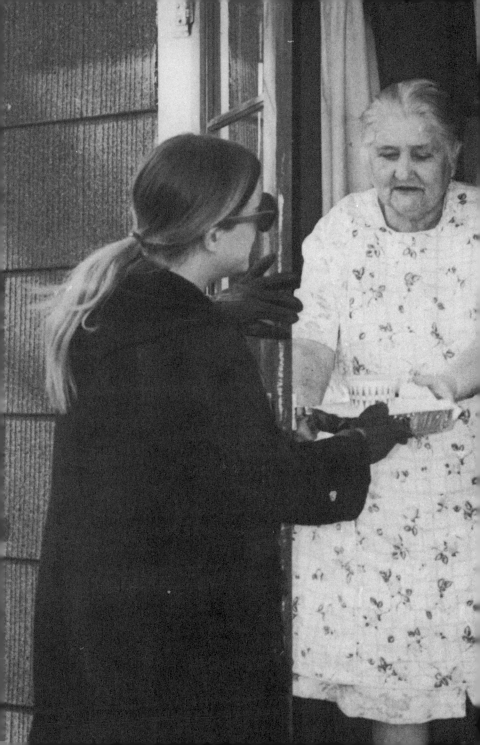

Step Three:
Have a Learning Session with Jesus

Jesus summons the burdened and heavy laden. "Come to me . . . take my yoke upon you, and learn from me." He promises, "You will find rest" (Matt. 11:28-29).

He who bore the heaviest of all burdens said, "My yoke is easy, and my burden is light" (Matt. 11:30).

His supreme delight was to be in the Father's will. "My food is to do the will of him who sent me" (John 4:34). The Father's will was his constant concern. "I seek not my own will but the will of him who sent me" (John 5:30). The Father's will was his easy yoke and light burden. The hot tears of Gethsemane became glistening diamonds: "thy will, not mine, be done."

For us, too, the gentle yoke of the Father's will lightens our burdens. The "he's not heavy, he's my brother" attitude gives wings to burdens. When we know that the burden we are bearing is the Father's will for us, drudgery becomes delight.

Jesus knew his mission: "The Son of Man himself has not come to be served but to serve, and to give his life to set many others free" (Mark 10:45 PHILLIPS). At the outset of his public ministry he announced his program: "To preach good news to the poor," "to proclaim release to the captives and recovering of sight to the blind," "to set at liberty those who are oppressed" (Luke 4:18).

In the Gospels Jesus is seen stooping down to people, mending their hurts, healing their diseases, and helping in their needs.

There is breathless awe in the report, "As many as touched [the fringe of his garment] were made well" (Matt. 14:36). "Many followed him, and he healed them all" (Matt. 12:15). Luke records sensitively, "When the crowds learned it; they followed him; and he welcomed them and spoke to them of the kingdom of God, and cured those who had need of healing" (Luke 9:11).

Jesus had a heart for people. Coming ashore in Galilee he saw a great crowd, "and he had compassion on them, and healed their sick" (Matt. 14:14).

Outside Jericho, surrounded by a throng, Jesus spotted two blind men standing at a distance. He stopped and called them and restored their sight.

His love went deep. One person ran up to him, "Lord, he who you love is ill"; "He was deeply moved in spirit"; "Jesus wept" (John 11:3, 33, 35).

In every sense Jesus was the man for others. He didn't think of himself. His working schedule reached exhaustion levels. Disturbed by his consuming pace, his relatives "set out to take charge of him" (Mark 3:21 NEB). They said, in effect, "Stop, man, you're killing yourself!" His answer:

"We must work the works of him who sent me, while it is day" (John 9:4). "My Father has never yet ceased his work, and I am working too" (John 5:17 NEB).

Today, as always, Jesus is at work among his people. His concern to serve them has not diminished. The kingdom cause remains nearest his heart. Today and every day, he is saving "those who approach God through him; he is always living to plead on their behalf" (Heb. 7:25 NEB).

Jesus has not changed. He loved and served people when he walked on earth. He loves and serves them day by day from his throne on high.

If an eminent doctor were to concern himself with our sickness and offer his help, we would be delighted. How exciting to know that our heavenly Physician and Helper loves and serves us!

"Abide in my love," Jesus said (John 15:9). We continue his work of loving and caring. Through us Christ reaches down in tenderness to earth's poor creatures and draws them to himself.

We too have a ministry of healing and helping. God says, "Pray for one another, that you may be healed" (James 5:16).

We place ourselves and others into his hands. "Thy will be done," we pray, counting on his deeper love and higher wisdom. He knows, better than we, whether he will be more glorified in our healing or in our sickness.

He has taught us to pray, in all circumstances, "Thy will, not mine, be done." This is the gentle yoke that lightens the load.

Step Four:
Fulfill a Productive Prayer Ministry

The telephone has put the world at our fingertips. If we had the call numbers, we could communicate with 419 million people. In the U.S. 162 million phones are used for 220 billion calls annually.

Prayer communications are even more amazing. Without lifting a receiver or dialing a number we can communicate with the Lord of the universe. The line is never busy. Never are we put on hold. Every prayer of faith is answered in one of three ways: Yes, no, wait.

Jesus offers generous prayer promises:

"Whatever you ask in my name, I will do it" (John 14:13).

"If you ask anything in my name, I will do it" (John 14:14).

"If you ask anything of the Father, he will give it to you in my name" (John 16:23).

"Whatever you ask the Father in my name, he will give it to you" (John 15:16 PHILLIPS).

"Ask, and you will receive, that your joy may be full" (John 16:24).

There's power in the name of Jesus. The devil quails when a believer takes authority over a bad situation in the mighty name of Jesus.

By invoking the name of Jesus and pleading the promises we can fulfill a productive prayer ministry. Dwight L. Moody said, "Tarry at his promises and God will meet you there."

Jesus said, "He who believes in me will also do the works that I do" (John 14:12). In John 12 he promises to give us his words, his works, his peace, his joy, his love, his glory. God has linked his working with our praying. Through prayer we do his work in every part of the globe: We work on the international scene by praying for the heads of state in the interest of world peace as God commands (1 Tim. 2:1).

We work on the missionary front as God commands. "Pray . . . the Lord of harvest to send out laborers into his harvest" (Matt. 9:38).

We work in the wake of massive disasters in distant parts of the world. Never need we say, "There's nothing I can do about the problem." Not true! We can always do the best that can be done: we can pray. After we pray, we aspire to match prayers with actions.

Visiting a church member in the hospital, a pastor said, "Lucy, be sure to make the best of your time while you're here in the hospital."

With a quizzical look Lucy asked: "What can I possibly do here confined between two sheets?"

The pastor explained: "You can fulfill a rich ministry of prayer through which you will draw down God's blessings upon missionaries, imprisoned and suffering Christians, and many other people and causes."

Lucy's eyes were opened to the vision of a great ministry of loving Christian service through prayer. On his second visit the pastor detected a glow of triumph in her eyes. "Pastor," she said, "I want to thank you for what you've done for me. You've changed my self-pity into a self-giving ministry of loving service to others. This has brought a delightful feeling of usefulness. Hours and days of weariness have become hours and days of cheerfulness. I have experienced the joy that comes with loving service to others "

If, through prayer, we are able to draw down God's blessings upon many people and causes, it doesn't speak well of us if we don't. There's a sharp rebuke in a little-known Bible verse: "Far be it from me that I should sin against the Lord by ceasing to pray for you" (1 Sam. 12:23).

Older folk have more time on their hands after retirement than ever before. They're in a position to fulfill a distinguished and productive prayer ministry. They realize that Satan's whisper, suggesting that there is nothing worthwhile for us to do, is phony. Years of retirement, even with some physical limitations, may in fact be years of rich

73

fruit bearing and heroic achievement. God says, "They still bring forth fruit in old age" (Ps. 92:14).

Senior citizens ought to reorient their attitude from sunset to sunrise, from reaching an end to reaching a beginning. Though strength and health are waning, they're headed for the fountain of eternal health and strength.

SECRET SERVICE

If the shut-ins all united
     In one voice of common prayer,
What a ceaseless shower of blessing
     Should be falling everywhere!
Though so weak and oftimes helpless,
     They can wield a mighty power
Lifting up their souls' petition
     To the Savior hour by hour.
They can importune the Father
     From the "secret place," and then,
In the quiet and the stillness,
     They can hear him speak to them.
Never soldier in fierce conflict
     Could a higher honor bring
Than the shut-in who's performing
     "Secret service" for the King!

Martin Luther found a letter in his mailbox with these words:

Dear Sir,

I know that you have a rich ministry of daily prayer. My problem is that I run out of thoughts and words. Can you help me?

This was Luther's answer:

Dear Friend in Christ,

I can't tell you how to pray, but I can tell you how I pray.

I usually follow the pattern of the Lord's Prayer. That is, I have a separate prayer on each phrase. After the phrase "Our Father who art in heaven" I say "My dear Father in heaven, I am thankful that I can address you as Father. I don't deserve this honor, but in your Word you said "To them that received him . . . he gives the right to become children of God.' I do believe in Jesus as my Savior, and I believe with all my heart that I am your dear child. I must confess, however, that I don't always act as your child. Sometimes I act like an orphan, as though I had no loving Father. Forgive me this sin, and grant through the Holy Spirit that I may call you Father with delight." Then I go on and do the same with the remaining phrases of the Lord's Prayer. After that I pray my way through the Ten Commandments, with a separate prayer on each commandment.

Time permitting, I follow the same pattern with each phrase of the Apostle's Creed.

Sometimes, while so engaged, the Holy Spirit breaks in and says: "Now, Martin, you've talked long enough. You be quiet for awhile and let me talk." When that happens, I listen intently and learn more in five minutes than I can write down in five hours.

Luther shared with us the secret of his zeal for prayer: "Prayer is a powerful thing, for God has bound and tied himself thereto." This was his daily rule: "I will not speak to man until I have first spoken to God. Nor do anything with my hand until I have been on my knees; nor read any letters or papers until I have read the Holy Scriptures; nor undertake much work without corresponding prayer. After prayer the Lord seems to set a holy dew upon my soul."

By means of prayer the Holy Spirit fills the soul with joyful positives, heading off nagging negatives.

Lord, what a change within one short hour
Spent in Thy presence will prevail to make—
What heavy burdens from our bosoms take!
What parched grounds refresh,
    as with a shower!
We kneel, and all around us seems to lower;
We rise, and all the distant and the near
Stand forth in sunny outline, brave and clear;

We kneel how weak, we rise how full of power!
Why therefore, should we do ourselves
   this wrong,
Or others—that we are not always strong;
That we are ever overborne with care;
That we should ever weak and heartless be,
Anxious or troubled, when with us is prayer,
And joy, and strength, and courage,
   are with Thee?

RICHARD CHENEVIX TRENCH

Sir Thomas Browne, a beloved English physician wrote: "I have resolved to pray always and in all places. I pray upon the sight of any church that God may be worshipped there in spirit, and that many souls may be saved there; I pray daily for my sick patients and for the patients of other physicians. When I enter a home I pray that the peace of God may abide there. After hearing a sermon I pray for God's blessing upon all who have heard and upon the messenger who has spoken. I pray for healthy persons that God may beautify them within. Upon the sight of a deformed person I pray that God may give him holiness of soul and at last the healing of the resurrection."

Step Five: By Love Serve One Another

They who give themselves to a ministry of love and service to others make an amazing discovery:

78

their gloom clouds disappear; sunlight floods the spirit.

Faith brings us to God; love makes us like God, for God is love. The godliest thing we can ever do is to love.

The Bible uses a special word to express God''s extraordinary kind of love. The word is *agape*. *Agape* love is a special kind of love. It embraces even the unlovable.

Our kind of love often ceases when the object of love is no longer attractive. When we have *agape* love, we love others not because of what *they* are but because of what *we* are.

Of the person who believes in him Jesus said, "Out of his heart shall flow rivers of living water" (John 7:38). The water of life and love "Love is of God, and he who loves is born of God" (1 John 4:7).

God implants his love in us. "God's love has flooded our inmost heart through the Holy Spirit he has given us" (Rom. 5:5 NEB).

We express God's love because it is within us. All we need to do is to live out what God has given us and to be in life what we are in faith. God demands nothing of us except on the ground of what we are and have by his grace.

Henry Drummond, author of *The Greatest Thing in the World,* makes a promising proposal: "Every day for three weeks read St. Paul's Ode of Love—1 Corinthians, Chapter 13. Put to practice as faithfully as you can all that it demands. I guarantee that it will transform your life."

Dr. Karl Menninger, the eminent Christian psychiatrist, resolved to test his theory that "love is the medicine of the world." He directed his hospital staff—doctors, therapists, nurses, office workers—to make every contact with patients a love contact. Hospitalization time was cut in half. The noted doctor came to this conclusion: "Love is the key to the entire therapeutic program of the modern psychiatric hospital."

Jim Kasten, a young man of sterling Christian character, died of cancer at the age of 26. When I visited Jim on Easter Sunday, 1981, I asked his nurse, "Is Jim a good patient?"

"He's the best patient in the hospital," she answered. Members of the hospital staff, who for six weeks observed Jim's radiant faith, agreed.

In a letter Jim shared the secret of his strong faith and fervent love. "Every day I find comfort in knowing that God is in control of my life. This gives me a feeling of peace and contentment. I would like to share with the whole world what God means to me. He is my best friend. I wouldn't give him up for anything."

Jim's beautiful ministry of love during those trying days will be lovingly remembered by his family and friends.

Where *agape* love prevails, life becomes a joyful adventure, even when onslaughts of pain and agony are intense.

Jesus, who knew more about life than anyone else, said in effect, "Serve self, lose self; give self away, find self."

Self-service has few rewards, none lasting. Even though it be only a cup of water given to a child, serving others will not lose its reward.

An infallible recipe for being miserable is to dote on self, pamper self, fill self with self. We find fulfillment and happiness in loving service to others. Saints discover their stature in stooping low to lift others high.

Children at play say, "Finders keepers, losers weepers." Jesus says the opposite, "Finders weepers, losers keepers." "He who loses his life for my sake will find it" (Matt. 10:39).

The happiest, healthiest people are they who give themselves in loving service to others. Spiritually, psychologically, biologically, the principle holds true: love or die

Tribulation's tears soften us to concern for others. "God comforts us in all our troubles, so that we in turn may be able to comfort others in any trouble of theirs and to share with them the consolation we ourselves receive from God" (2 Cor. 1:4 NEB).

Archibald MacLeish has a sobering comment: "The crime against life, the worst of all crimes, is

not to feel. . . . There perhaps was never a civilization in which a kind of torpor, of lethargy, of apathy, the snake-like sin of coldness-of-heart, was commoner than now. . . . None of us is safe from it."

To lose the joy of loving and caring makes us abjectly poor. Going our own sweet way, with no regard for the burdened, the poor, and the needy, is a dubious kind of luxury. God is always nudging his children to have a heart for others. This brings enrichment undreamed of. This is God's promise, "If you really fulfil the royal law, according to the scripture, 'You shall love your neighbor as yourself,' you do well" (James 2:8). Love is twice blessed: it blesses him who gives and him who receives.

Sadhu Sundar Singh, famous evangelist of India, was walking to Tibet on the Himalayan snow when he was overtaken by a snowstorm. As he was running for shelter, he was joined by a fellow traveler. Together, they came across a man lying in the snow. Sundar Singh suggested that they carry the man, who was dying of cold. But the stranger ran away saying, "I must save *my* life!" With great difficulty, Sundar Singh carried the dying man, and at some distance away came upon the stranger lying in the path frozen to death. By the rubbing of the bodies, Sundar Singh and his companion renewed their circulation, obtained warmth, and reached a place of safety.

We are never wrong if we follow love's way;
we are always wrong if we don't.

Step Six:
Give Yourself to Praise and Worship

To its first question, "What is the chief end
of man?" the Westminster Shorter Catechism
gives this good and true answer: "To glorify God
and enjoy him forever."

The supreme use of life is to worship and
praise God. God comes before his work. Before
we do the work of the Lord we offer praise and
thanksgiving to the Lord of the work.

In worship we reach life's highest level. Our
noblest work is to adore. Many things we do are
means to ends. Worship is an end in itself, the
beginning of an eternal activity.

Worship and praise dispel worry and fretting.
The smiles of people with disabilities, of sufferers
and shut-ins, are the incense of praise rising
heavenward.

The Apostle John wrote to his friend Gaius:
"My heartfelt prayer for you, my very dear friend,
is that you may be as healthy and prosperous in
every way as you are in soul" (3 John 2 PHILLIPS).

Though his physical health was waning, Gaius
was hale and hearty in soul. By the victory of faith
spiritual life remains strong even when the body
grows weak.

In his desire to collect fine violins, Luigi Tarisia denied himself most pleasures of life. One morning he was found dead in his bare cottage. In his attic he had stored 246 exquisite violins. In blind devotion to violins the man robbed the world of the music held silent all those years.

Are we depriving God, ourselves, and others of praise and thanksgiving?

Some linguists say that the word *thank* is related to the word *think*. Thinking leads to thanking. Thanking leads to many related virtues. The thankful heart is a joyful heart; a joyful heart offers praise; a heart full of praise is a heart full of good will.

"Give thanks in all circumstances" St. Paul recommends (1 Thess. 5:18). Henry Ward Beecher has an interesting illustration. "A thankless heart is like a hand drawn through the sand—no metallic substance clings to it. A thankful heart is like a magnet drawn through the sand—all kinds of metallic substances cling to it. The thankless heart finds little reason for thanksgiving. The thankful heart discovers many reasons for thanksgiving. It vibrates with joyful recognition of God's mercies."

A wagon train of pioneers was on the old Oregon Trail. Water was scarce, wagons broke down, the heat was stifling. A general feeling of fretfulness and faultfinding destroyed the early optimism and good cheer of the company. So it was decided to halt their journey and hold a council to air all their complaints and troubles.

As the people sat around the campfire glaring at one another, tempers were hot and harsh. Then one man arose and said: "Before we do anything else, I think we should first thank God that we have come this far with no loss of life, with no serious trouble with the Indians, and enough strength to finish the journey." Agreeing with the speaker, each one about the campfire thanked God for his protection. No complaints were made; things were seen in their proper perspective for the very first time. That is the transformation a thankful heart often makes.

George Allen, football coach, was asked, "Sir, why do you jog?"

He answered, "For the inspiration of it."

We praise God for his goodness; we magnify him for his mercy; we extol him for his greatness; we adore him for his love; we glorify him for his majesty; we thank him for his generosity; we love him for his grace. All this we do to please God and for the inspiration it gives.

Step Seven:
Keep a Firm Hand on Hope

Hope is "like an anchor for our lives, an anchor safe and sure" (Heb. 6:19 NEB). An anchor grips the bottom of the sea to hold the boat steady in

the lashing waves. Hope holds us steady and strong in the turbulent tides of life. It has positive power to overcome negative panic. Hope may be defined as faith stretched out. It stretches out over the entire expanse from here to eternity.

In faith we accept what God says about things that are real and things that are unreal. "The things that are seen are transient, but the things that are unseen are eternal" (2 Cor. 4:18). We believe that this affirmation is true. Many people today consider it pure nonsense. To them nothing is real unless they can see it, eat it, bank it, ride in it, or hug it. They are wrong; God is right. The future will manifest the difference between their hopeless end and our endless hope.

God's Word vibrates with sounds of hope. In it there are tons of buoyant hope and victory, not an ounce of defeatism.

Hope is one of the three cardinal virtues, along with faith and love. It is the most shortchanged of the three. For this we forfeit victory and prosperity.

"Where there is life there is hope," we usually say. God says in effect: "Where there is hope there is life." This we are sure of, where there is no hope, there is no life. For happiness it is essential to know what will happen to us in the future, and where we will spend eternity.

Christianity has a forward look. For us, all the trumpets are sounding on the other side. Psychiatry traces life backward. Christianity traces life forward.

The goal of life is more than a plot in the cemetery. It is an eternal home in the house of many mansions.

Paul had this prayer for his Christian friends: "I pray that your inward eyes may be illumined, so that you may know what is the hope to which he calls you, what the wealth and glory of the share he offers you among his people in their heritage" (Eph. 1:18 NEB).

For us who are believers the future grows brighter by the hour. Every step is a step toward home. We are living on the doorstep of eternal health and happiness. The present may be bleak. the future is bright.

Helmut Gollwitzer, who with his friends faced dreadful terrors in a Russian salve-labor camp, experienced hope's sustaining power. He wrote: "In spirit we put ourselves into the place of the early Christians. Like them, we bled under the lash of persecution; like them, we suffered bodily and mental anguish. And like them we stood firm. Like them, we know we would have an eternal life with Christ in glory. That hope held us firm. It gave meaning to our otherwise miserable existence. During day hours and before going to sleep we thought a thousand times of the reception awaiting us in our heavenly home. This hope was the burden of every conversation, of every thought, of every prayer. The present had little value. Only the future had meaning. 'One day less!' sighed everyone at day's end. 'One day closer to our heavenly home'!"

Pliny the Younger was directed by the Roman Senate to investigate the sect known as Christians, suspected of disloyalty to the government. He reported: "All I can find out about this sect called Christians is that they pray to one Jesus as God, they sing hymns, and they pay their taxes."

How quickly and spontaneously those early Christians—almost constantly under fire—broke out into song! The hope of their eternal inheritance with Christ in heaven caused unbounded rejoicing.

The Christian religion is a religion of joy. It was born in song. At the Savior's birth angels poured out of heaven with the song of great joy for all people. Christians have been singing ever since. They have much to sing about: an eternal home with Chirst in heaven.

This hope sets the spirit ablaze with joy beyond telling, happiness beyond describing.

A Christian and an unbeliever were walking down a country road. "I have no fear of death," the unbeliever said.

The Christian asked, "But do you have any hope in death?"

The unbeliever's answer was honest but grim: "I have no hope."

The supreme tragedy of life is to suffer the death from which Christ came to set us free.

The supreme triumph of life is to walk through the gate of death into life eternal. The triumphant hope, which is faith stretched out to the very end, gives us authority to exult, "O death, where is thy victory? O death, where is thy sting?" (1 Cor. 15:55).

Death, the old serpent's son, once had a sting of hell and burning fire. No more. Our triumphant Lord snatched the keys of hell out of death"s hand.

Death, once so dreadful, is now a harmless thing, a porter at the gate of life. It signals the beginning, not the end; sunrise, not sunset; victory, not defeat. It offers life's supreme adventure; entrance through its portals into the presence of God.

He whom we love most, and who loves us most, will welcome us home.

John writes: "Beloved, we are God's children now; it does not yet appear what we shall be, but we know that when he appears, we shall be like him, for we shall see him as he is" (1 John 3:2).

At his coming he will bring in a new heaven and a new earth. The curse will be lifted. Primordial glory will be restored.

But the renovation of the cosmos is not the focus of New Testament expectancy. It is rather the appearance of a Person. The very Person whom St. Paul addresses as "Christ Jesus our hope" (1 Tim. 1:1).

This will happen when he comes: "The Lord himself will descend from heaven. . . . And the dead in Christ will rise first; then we who are alive, who are left, shall be caught up together with them in the clouds to meet the Lord . . . so we shall always be with the Lord" (1 Thess. 4:16-17).

The book of Revelation describes this dramatic scene: "The seventh angel blew his trumpet, and there were loud voices in heaven, saying: 'The kingdom of the world has become the kingdom of our Lord and of his Christ, and he shall reign for ever and ever' " (Rev. 11:15).

Two sentences summarize the essential message of Revelation: Satan will put up a furious fight. Christ will win the victory. As King of kings and Lord of lords, he rules for ever and ever.

As in Shakespeare's exquisite line, "Journeys end in lovers meeting," even so in the romance of redemption the travail of time ends in the meeting of lovers.

"So we shall always be with the Lord," is God's solemn promise. This golden hope lightens heavy hearts and brightens dark paths. Headaches and heartaches are gone forever. Bitter agonies have turned into sweet ecstasies, crosses into crowns, teardrops into diamonds. Every prospect glows with dazzling glory. Jesus' prayer is answered, "Father, I desire that they also, whom thou hast given me, may be with me where I am, to behold my glory" (John 17:24). In tender expectancy the spirit calls, "Make haste, my beloved" (Song of Sol. 8:14). He is on his way now to take his children home. When he arrives, the universe will tremble in awesome wonder as the glory unfolds.

Nail-pierced hands, take the scepter!
Bruised feet, ascend the throne!
Bleeding head, wear the crown!
Thine is the kingdom and the power and the
glory forever.

And because it is his, it is ours, too. Glory, hallelujah!